A Winter Walk

ANGUS MACIVER

First published in 2024 by Angus Maciver

Copyright © Angus Maciver 2024

ISBN: 978-1-3999-8042-5

Typeset by Palimpsest Book Production Ltd, Falkirk, Stirlingshire

Printed by Print Force, Lancaster Way, Stratton Business Park,
Biggleswade SG18 8TQ

PREFACE

When it was announced in October 1980 that the West Highland Way was now opened as an official long distance footpath, it gave me the challenge I had been looking for. It had been a few years since I had done any long distance walking so I knew that it would involve some planning and perhaps most of all training. At an early stage I also touted my climbing/walking friends to see if they would join me on this venture but no one had the time available over Xmas or New Year.

Ron Kirkpatrick however came to the rescue by saying that he could join me on Hogmanay wherever I would be at that stage. The plan was finalised, I would leave on Boxing Day, giving myself an average walking day of 13 miles which seemed reasonable for the time of year and knowing how dirty the weather could be. Ron would join me at Kingshouse and we would spend the last two days together finishing at Fort William on Friday 2nd January 1981.

The weather before Xmas was very wet. One low pressure area followed another, sweeping in from the Atlantic in a mainly SW direction. Suddenly on Xmas Eve a change took place. The wind backed NW and with a low pressure area centred near Iceland it meant that the rain was now turning mainly to sleet and snow.

Xmas Day dawned and it was raining in Falkirk. I enjoyed a quiet day at home with the family. Late afternoon saw me preparing to have a jog only to be told that it was chucking it out of the heavens. This time it was hail and sleet, so I sat down to await an improvement in the weather. The sleet turned to snow and it blew hard for an hour before abating. I finally hit the road and jogged on snow covered pavements for 45 minutes.

I phoned Ron to bring him up to date with my thoughts and plans. The weather was not promising and I did want to avoid a first day soaking so I was prepared to cancel my first day and start the second from Drymen. Ron agreed that it seemed the sensible thing to do. It was just as well our other friend Archie was not managing this trip or it would be all systems go bad weather or not. By 11pm the sky had cleared and a hard frost had set in, so things seemed reasonable for a start in the morning.

ACKNOWLEDGEMENTS

I would like to thank Rick Goater for his comments and suggestions with the text of this book. His knowledge and experience made this book possible.

A Winter Walk
WEST HIGHLAND WAY

26th December 1980 – 2nd January 1981

by ANGUS MACIVER

DAY 1

I awoke at 0745 and turned on the radio to catch the weather forecast.

From my bed I could hear the traffic on the avenue crackling on the ice so I knew that the roads would be difficult to negotiate.

The forecast was not good. Showers of hail, sleet or snow was covering most of the country. I decided to stay put meantime. By 10am the sun was shining on a snow covered landscape. Looking to the north I could see the Ochil Hills and the mountains further away.

A decision was made swiftly; I would go by car to near Drymen cutting out the initial stage of the walk through the Blane valley.

My wife Janet and daughter Anne came with me so that the car would be left at home.

The roads locally were covered with ice and driving was hazardous but once on to the motorway we were soon speeding along towards Stirling.

The surrounding scene was beautiful. How snow enhances the hills and surrounding countryside.

We arrived at Gartness road end just after midday and I bid farewell to Janet and Anne.

Anne's encouraging last remark was that I must be mad.

Heavy snow showers were now around Loch Lomond as I started out down the road to pick up the West Highland Way where it leaves the old railway line to follow the road to Drymen.

I reached the railway bridge and peered over into a water logged pathway. Thank goodness I had missed that part; a boat would have been of more use.

It was pleasant walking so far. My rucksack seems not to be heavy although I know that a 40lb plus load would tell sooner or later.

By 1.30pm I had reached Gateside near Drymen and ahead the snow clouds loomed menacingly. I sheltered behind a gatepost and had lunch. Lunch consisted of two rolls with cold meat and some chocolate.

The blizzard swirled around me for some time before I decided that I was getting too cold and that I would be warmer on the move, snow or no snow.

A movement on the tree in front caught my attention, a Treecreeper hunting for food in all the nooks and crannies made me forget the weather for a moment.

On the move again, this time dressed like an Arctic explorer. I had even put on my Snow goggles so as not to be blinded by the swirling snow around me. By the time I had reached the main road and Blarnavaid Farm the blizzard had gone.

I stripped off my waterproofs and continued up into the Garadhban forest. The path was wet and boggy at first where it crossed farm land but once into the forest proper the path was good. The snow being fresh was balling up underneath the insteps of my boots making walking a bit of a nuisance.

It was now glorious all around. The view was improving with each step, both behind me and to the west where I could see glimpses of Loch Lomond coming into view. I took several photographs to record this.

Several Bullfinches came down through the trees to the roadside to meet me. Their soft piping calls keeping them in touch with each other.

I crossed the Drymen to Gartmore road and climbed higher into the forest. I met two young ladies out for a walk, said hello and passed on.

Another bird appeared on my right. This time a wood-pecker, flying away with it's very conspicuous flight. It seemed too large for a Great Spotted so could possibly have been a Green. A note or call would have been helpful in sorting that problem out.

The sky was now darkening so I began to look for a place to camp for the night.

A skein of geese appeared from nowhere, wheeled as they saw me and drifted away towards their likely roost at the Endrick Mouth.

I had now reached the edge of the forest near Moorpark and found a suitable spot to erect my tent. Someone had built a rough shelter with a piece of corru-gated metal and it was fitted out with two car seats.

I pitched my tent nearby and settled in for the night.

At 8.04pm I became aware of the wind howling outside. My first night light is half way through already so my stock won't last long.

Time 9.30pm and I have settled down finally for the

night after a short walk along a woodland path. A glorious sky tonight, stars by the million and not a snow cloud in sight.

Looking towards Glasgow the sky is bright orange whilst in the sky above Orion seems to stand guard. I offered a silent prayer for a fine days walking forecast for tomorrow.

Approach to Conic Hill

DAY 2

I awakened at 8am after a cold, sleep disturbed night. I had found it difficult to sleep which is unusual for me. During the night I heard a fox barking several times and a Tawny Owl called from nearby.

The morning was calm and windless which augured well for the climb over Conic Hill to Balmaha.

The snow was crisp underfoot as I started out on my days walking. A Great Spotted Woodpecker called 'kek kek' as if to say, good morning it was me you saw yesterday.

Another small bird flitted out from low down on my left, flew in front of me and perched on a small bush to my right. I was rather surprised to see that it was a Reed Bunting hunting a forest area 600 feet or so above sea level.

As the forest road ended and footpath began a Common Snipe flew from under my feet and zig zagged away into the sky in front of me.

The path continued out onto Moor Park and walking became difficult in the snow which in some places was a foot deep. On the approach to Conic Hill three Red Grouse took off and flew a short distance on whirring wings.

This section of the official guide describing the ascent of Conic Hill is very accurate. Even with no bracken to hide guide posts the line of the walk can be misunderstood. With snow covering the long heather this proved a tough slog with a heavy pack.

I reached Balmaha at last and visited the local shop to purchase the margarine that I had left at home.

Beyond Balmaha the island of Inchcailloch came into view and I was rewarded by a male Sparrowhawk chasing tits along the water's edge.

I visited the cairn where the plaque to announce the opening of the walk in October 1980.

After a lunch break I continued along the loch side which turned out to be generally uneventful, just a matter of slogging out the miles through a variety of woodland to reach Rowardennan which had been planned as my next stopping place. During the afternoon several species of bird were observed. Jay, Mistle Thrush, and Long tailed Tit.

As it was now 5pm and hence dark I pitched my tent at the loch side beyond the Forestry Commission car park. After a coffee I went back to the public phone to phone home only to find it out of order. Fortunately the hotel bar was open and the young man in attendance kindly let me use the hotel public phone. I returned to the bar with its huge log fire, bought a pint of beer and just relaxed.

It was now raining steadily and I thought ahead to tomorrow, wondering what was in store for me.

Highland boundary fault from Conic Hill

West Highland Way cairn Balmaha

DAY 3

I spent an uncomfortable night camped at the lochside. The wind veered North West and it blew hard all night with rain and snow showers falling intermittently. I had borrowed my tent from another friend called Archie, and was not sure how it would behave in a strong gale force wind and that made me rather anxious to the point of not sleeping but just hanging on to the tent poles.

As it turned out the tent performed well. Saunders can be congratulated for the design of their Dolomite tent. I should have realised also that if the tent belonged to my friend Archie it would have to perform well in all weathers.

I dozed off and on through the night with the result that I slept till 9.30am.

Looking out the tent gave me courage for another days walking. The sky was wild, but interspersed with patches of blue sky and it was not raining.

I ate breakfast as quickly as possible and struck camp.

On passing Ptarmigan Lodge I decided to stay on the high forestry road that runs to near the bothy at Rowchoish. This would allow me to try and make up some of the time that I had lost earlier in the day.

The West Highland Way path runs along the loch side at this section.

After having walked for an hour I had to stop to attend to the heel of my left foot which had blistered the previous day.

Running repairs done I hurried on, stopping a little later to look at some wild goats on the path side.

I took out my camera to take a picture but rather too slowly as the goats had trotted off up the hillside where they merged perfectly with the trees with the exception of a white nanny.

I was now feeling in good fettle and was feeling so warm that I was soon in shirt sleeves to try and keep cool. I soon reached the end of the metal road and I took out some lunch (Yorkie bar, apple, tangerine) stuffed them in my pockets and ate as I walked.

On reaching Cailness I stopped at a little burn which had a blue plastic cup hanging from a hook on a post. This was a wonderful gesture by the person responsible and made me think how simple things in life give the most satisfaction.

I suddenly realised at this stage that my right heel was bothering me so out came my first aid kit and applied a plaster to it.

I reached Inversnaid Hotel by 2pm where I sampled their lager. However their Alsatian dog after giving me a fright proved quite a friendly beast. I was once bitten by a dog of that breed so it makes you rather wary of them.

I was soon on the trail again and honestly not looking forward to what the guide says is the roughest part of the walk.

On completing it I would definitely agree with that description.

If I had a complaint to make about the walk so far it would be that branches of trees over hanging the path be cut slightly back to allow people with 40lb packs to stay upright instead of having to go on hands and knees every so often.

I feel this would in no way spoil the rugged nature of the path at this section. The main hazard I encountered was a waterfall which had to be climbed. I could not recollect reading about it beforehand but perhaps I missed it out. It was a tricky situation because on the left there was a drop of some 10 feet into Loch Lomond.

One had to forget about water pouring on you and look for hand and foot holds.

My destination was intended as Inverarnan but I realised I would not make that today as the light was fading fast and I had to make camp whilst I could still see.

My torch doesn't seem to have much power left and in retrospect should have had a spare battery with me. I stopped finally ½ a mile south of Doune.

I was soaked through mainly with sweat although there had been some rain during the day as well. I tried out for the first time a muscle rub called 'Deep Heat'. It certainly eased my shoulders and legs and stopped them from stiffening up.

I made some tea, laced it with a few drops of whisky and lay back to snooze.

At 8pm I awoke and decided my stomach needed attention. I made myself a meal of bacon, sausage and potato followed by some instant custard with coffee to follow.

The weather now seemed a little calmer or perhaps I had selected a more sheltered spot than last night.

My plan for tomorrow is to rise early and get on the move when the light is good as I have to make up some distance that I lost today. My destination tomorrow is Tyndrum where I have promised to call on Mr & Mrs Music at the caravan site beside the lower station whom I have come to know this past couple of years.

Birds seen today were: Blue tit, long tailed tit, Dipper, Blackbird, Carrion Crow and 5 Goosanders.

PS. I have read the guide again to find that my water-fall does get a mention after all and that the path goes up to avoid it. If all else fails read the instructions.

DAY 4

I slept reasonably well last night and woke to some wind and rain but nothing to talk about.

I had set my alarm for 7am but actually woke at 6.40am. Breakfast was quickly made and consumed by 7.30am and I waited for dawn.

The weather this morning was rather blustery with heavy rain. Its direction was south westerly made me realise that I was in for a wet days walking.

The path towards Inverarnan was not too difficult to find or negotiate. I reached Beinn Glas farm by midday and shortly afterwards met a shepherd gathering in a flock of sheep off the hill.

He was decked out in a fine set of waterproofs which he certainly needed as the rain was now incessant.

I was by now getting wet throughout and the temperature with the strong winds made me feel quite chilly. I had lunch again whilst on the move due to several factors, rain, cold and lack of any shelter in this lower section of Glen Falloch.

The river Falloch was turbulent and flowing very fast due to the heavy rain. As I approached Derrydaroch a Buzzard appeared over the main road and flew over the river before disappearing from view. I thought it quite unusual to see such a bird flying in such atrocious conditions.

On reaching the main road and I made a decision to go into Crianlarich and find a bed and breakfast establishment.

I was by now really cold and I regretted the decision to try wearing my cotton/polymid tracksuit top under my waterproof jacket.

I looked at the sheep around me and it somehow confirmed in my mind that I should be wearing wool.

On reaching Crianlarich I found some initial difficulty in finding somewhere suitable for bed and breakfast but on visiting the Benmore restaurant the proprietor phoned the Allt Chaorain guest house to arrange a bed for me.

I left the restaurant in heavy driving rain to walk the 1.1/2 miles to the Allt Chaorain but after a half mile a Volvo car stopped to enquire if I was the gentleman who had been in the Benmore restaurant. Somewhat staggered I said "yes". Here was real hospitality, my host Mr Blackie out looking for me to save me walking in the rain.

Allt Chaorain House is all you would wish for in a bed and breakfast. The proprietor was a friendly host, good food and a comfortable well-furnished house.

Mr Blackie seemingly is well used to climbers and very willingly took away all my wet clothes to dry them out.

Dinner that night was super and consisted of home-made soup with cream, smoked ham, peach, lettuce, tomato, green beans and boiled potatoes. The sweet was ice cream with Christmas pie. Coffee was served in the lounge afterwards.

Outside I could still hear the rain but the forecast promises showers and perhaps bright intervals. The temperature is to go down also.

I telephoned home to report on my travels and tribulations. There was nothing new to report from home.

My feet tonight are feeling the effects of four days carrying a pack, sore, blistered here and there and generally aching. If I have to continue tomorrow the first aid kit will need to be out in the morning. During the evening I had a pleasant conversation with Ian Blackie the proprietor of the Allt Chaorain guest house as it had turned out that he used to bank with a good friend of mine whilst he lived and worked in Leith Edinburgh.

Strathfillan looking to Ben More

DAY 5

I awoke at 8am, had breakfast at 8.30am after having a good night's sleep. I gathered together all of my gear which was nice and dry.

The strong wind and rain was still around so prospects seemed similar to yesterday for the days walking ahead of me.

I decided to phone ahead to the Bridge of Orchy Hotel and book a room for the night.

My walk started by using the A82 main road towards Tyndrum and after a while picked up the West Highland Way path where it crosses the road from the forestry plantation north west of Crianlarich and leads down towards the farm at Kirkton.

A good road runs along the Auchtertyre farm where I was greeted by two sheep dogs that on seeing me came racing along the road, much to the consternation of the shepherd who was whistling them back to him.

I stopped briefly to speak to two farm hands, jesting them about their well trained dogs.

The older man replied somewhat amusingly that the dogs had been confused with the apparition that had appeared on the road. I suppose I did appear rather unusual covered from head to foot in wool

hat, cagoule and gaiters whilst carrying a huge rucksack.

I bade them farewell and left the men climbing into
their land rover to go and bring their Tups off the hill.

I noticed a large gull which was in a field at the farm
and from all its field markings it looked like a Glaucous
gull, perhaps blown inland with the strong winds.

I toiled onwards to Tyndrum where I was looking
forward to calling in to see Lin and Jeane Music at the
Pine trees caravan site. They were at home thankfully
and we chatted over coffee. Jeane began to show me
her handicraft items which were oval tiles with hand
paintings relating to the West Highland Way. I ordered
one there and then which would remind me of my walk
that winter.

An hour passed quickly and it was time to be on the
move again. Passing through Tyndrum and on upwards
I came upon workmen installing what seemed to be
water tanks next to the burn that flows down to the
village. I have to divert around a large amount of gravel
that covered the old road at this point.

At the summit of the pass I came upon a Grey Heron
who had been disturbed by my approach. The wind
which was now gale force and the Heron had some
difficulty in flying away from me.

A little further on I reached a sheep creep which gives
you access under the railway line and connects up with
the old military road which then goes downhill towards
Auch.

As I emerged on the other side I startled nine red deer
including nine stags that were feeding close by.

My next bird to encounter was my first Kestrel of the

trip. It was a spectacular sight, wheeling and hovering in the windy conditions.

As I reached Auch farm a Common Buzzard appeared momentarily amongst the forestry plantation.

Auch itself was a sea of water with all roads and tracks ankle deep. I trudged the next mile or two with the wind and rain now in my face.

A little later I reached the old railway cottage that had been used by the Glasgow group of the Holiday Fellowship as a bothy for some years. Sadly there was no one at home and that disappointed me as I had hoped to have a look round with thoughts of using it with my friends at a later date.

I walked on and reached the bridge of Orchy hotel around 4pm where I met Angus McDonald, the manager. He booked me in and we chatted about mutual friends. We spoke too about the weather forecast for tomorrow which is still rather wild. strong winds, rain and snow.

I phoned Ron after dinner who confirmed that he was still coming and that he would meet me tomorrow evening at Kingshouse.

DAY 6

The wind howled outside all night and the morning brought hope or despair, I couldn't decide which.

The hotel that night was full of English climbers, all hoping and planning to get on to the mountains that surround Bridge of Orchy. I felt rather sorry for them as they had come all the way from the south to enjoy some winter climbing which now looked unlikely.

By 10 am I had made the decision to continue to Kingshouse even although it was snowing heavily and accompanied by a strong west to North West wind

I entered the forestry plantation, climbed over the stile and picked up an obvious path which went upwards through the trees.

The going was good although wet underfoot. After climbing several hundred feet I encountered 2 coal tits prospecting the long heather for food.

As I reached the summit of the Mam Carraigh I was greeted by several showers of hail and snow. The view would be spectacular in better weather conditions.

I descended quickly towards the Inveroran hotel and was welcomed into the bar by the proprietor Mrs Granville.

I chatted with some Glasgow folks who had a Danish

girl with them and after an hour I moved on to the icy wastes of the Rannoch Moor by way of Corrie Ba.

On reaching Ba Bridge I stopped for a few minutes to gather my breath and relieve the weight of my pack off my shoulders.

A little later in the lea of Meall a'Bhuiridh I watched a herd of some 80 red deer before resuming my journey towards Black Rock cottage. The wind was now blowing directly into my face which made it tough going.

I reached the Kingshouse Hotel at 4.30 pm and waited for Ron to appear. (Note; the hotel at this time was closed).

The gale continued to blow snow horizontal so I sheltered in the lea of the building and made myself some tea.

I could hear snow ploughs out on the main road putting down grit so hoped Ron would appear soon.

Ron appeared out of the darkness and we discussed our original plan to camp that night but decided to head down into Glencoe and look for a bed and breakfast.

As luck would have it we found a nice bed and breakfast called Dunire and were made welcome by Duncan and Irene McDonald.

We were invited to join their Hogmanay party and Duncan piped in the New Year as we danced outside in the snow. We eventually crawled into bed at 3.30am.

Ron on the Devils Staircase

Angus on the Devils Staircase

DAY 7

The weather was similar to yesterday although the wind was a little less strong.

We drove the car back up the glen to Altnafeidh where we parked it up with the plan to collect it later.

We took the path up and over the Devils staircase to Kinlochleven in a time of 2 hours 50 minutes. The sun shone for much of the day which allowed us to enjoy the spectacular scenery on this part of the walk.

We saw one or two red grouse during our walk but nothing else of note.

We arrived at Kinlochleven which was bleak with no hotels open and even the public toilets closed up.

Near the bottom of the track we came upon some Long Tailed Tits flitting about in some birch trees.

We looked around for a spot to erect our tent and decided to use a small area within a conifer plantation across the river from the British Aluminium factory.

Once the tent was erected we crawled inside, got into our sleeping bags and slept for a few hours.

We awoke to the sound of rain on the tent which is not unusual for this part of the world.

Later we went out to phone home to our respective families and contact Gavin Reid in Fort William that we were on schedule to visit him tomorrow night.

DAY 8

It rained all night which could only be described as torrential.

We both slept reasonably well and awoke at 7.30am. Our tent was beginning to weep rather badly and we could feel the ground underneath was getting wetter.

After a quick breakfast we departed at 0930 for our final day's walking through the Lairighmor.

The path follows the main road for a short distance before striking up the hillside for 800 feet before meeting up with the land rover track that goes through this remote glen towards Fort William.

We walked all day with the wind and rain in our faces, which was rather a trudge with the only thing of note being a motor cyclist on a scramble bike who suddenly appeared around a bend in the track and nearly knocked us over.

We reached Upper Achintore Fort William at 3.30pm and were greeted at the home of my friends Gavin and Morag Reid.

It wasn't long till we had a glass of whisky in our hand and after a hot bath and lovely meal we relaxed with our hosts for the rest of the evening chatting about all manner of things.

The following day Gavin kindly ran us back to Altnafeidh in Glencoe to collect our car for our return journey home to Dunblane and Falkirk.

The wind is still howling tonight but thankfully no walking tomorrow.

ABOUT THE AUTHOR

Angus was born in Maryhill Glasgow in April 1939. He was one of four sons, Donald, Angus, Neil and Bruce. Angus's grandfather, Donald came from Lewis to join the Glasgow Police, as many others did in the past.

Angus attended primary school in Shakespeare Street and then, North Kelvinside for his secondary education. Whilst at primary school Angus was taught Scottish Country and social ceilidh dancing. He was part of a demonstration group who performed at a concert in Gairbraid Hall in Maryhill. Little did he know at that time how this would become part of his social life as he got older. He joined the Lifebuoys and later the Boys Brigade where he was a member of the brass band in the 6th company in Maryhill. Angus was no great academic but managed to achieve above average marks in his final year at North Kelvinside. Leaving at 15 years of age, he joined the Post Office as a telegraph messenger in 1954.

In his young years Angus always had an interest in birds and his copy of *The Observer's Book of Birds* was rarely out of his hands. This interest gave him the impetus to explore his local environment in Maryhill, particularly the area around the River Kelvin and the nearby Botanic Gardens. With other boys of his age, he found much pleasure in cycling and together they formed a group that cycled far and wide around central Scotland, often spending overnight stops at youth hostels such as Loch Ard, Balquhidder, Ardgarten, Rowardennan, Strone, Wanlochhead, Crosbie, Glendevon, Whiting Bay and Lendrick.

At this time Angus joined a local club where his dancing skills were enhanced by learning to waltz, foxtrot etc. Part of his social life then led him to the dance floor in the St Andrews Hall on a Friday evening with many other youths of his age.

In 1953 the family moved from Maryhill, where they lived in a tenement building to the west end of the city, to an end terrace house in Sunnyside Drive Blairdardie. The family lived in this house for many years and on the death of his dad and then mum his younger brother Neil and wife June became the owners.

As Post Office employees, staff were allowed to attend Langside College in the south side of the city as day-release students. He was fortunate to have a Natural History teacher named Charles P. Cromar who had retired from Glenmore Lodge in the Cairngorm National Park. Charles had been involved in the running of the lodge as an outdoor centre and he brought to Langside his love of the countryside and, in particular, mountain-eering.

Whilst spending a residential week at Dalston Hall near Carlisle the students were given the opportunity to climb Helvellyn and the famous Striding Edge. Angus thoroughly enjoyed this outing, and this day was to shape his future activities in the outdoors. On his return to

Langside he engaged in a discussion with Charles Cromar about starting a climbing club at Langside. Sometime later it emerged that he had been in contact with the Education Department about this and that they had a member of staff who had a mountaineering son who was looking for the opportunity to be involved in this venture.

Ronnie Crawford was a well-known mountaineer in Glasgow who had been involved with the Glasgow Glenmore Mountaineering club and was looking for pastures new. Ronnie came to meet Angus and his colleague Alistair Beatson who were interested in forming a climbing club.

Ronnie introduced them to a flow chart that he had created with the headline MOUNTAINEERING. His day job as a draughtsman at Weir's in Cathcart in the south of the city was very evident that evening. Under the heading, he had a list of activities all relating to what he could teach. These were: Hillwalking, Map & compass skills, Rock climbing, Abseiling, Birdwatching, Mountain birds and flowers, Photography, Camping, Snow and Ice climbing and Learning how to use Outdoor Access codes for the countryside to avoid conflict with landowners.

It was always Ronnie's idea that the club would be a training ground for budding mountaineers who would move on to other clubs after a few years. Eventually the Langside College club lost the use of the building. They then changed the name to Langside Mountaineering Club, which is still in existence today (2023) at Queens Park near Pollokshaws Road.

On reaching 17 years of age Angus was aware he would have to serve National Service in the armed services. As his father was a shipwright with Yarrow and Company in Scotstoun, he chose to spend it in the Royal Navy. Angus took himself off to the Clyde division of the RNVR at HMS *Graham* at 140 Whitefield Road Govan to enable him to join the Royal Navy for National Service. He was so keen to do this that he tried to join up one week before his 17th birthday, but he had to attend the following week instead! After undertaking drill and parade training, he joined the Radar Plot division for his first year.

At Langside, the climbing club was growing in size with other students joining. Many of them were Post Office staff and nursery nurses who also attended the college at that time. The next two years at Langside was all about honing the skills that Ronnie Crawford and his girlfriend Margaret Stewart shared. On Wednesday evenings they were taught rope skills, which included belaying, knots and climbing skills on the large wall bars. Map and compass skills were also on the agenda. At weekends, particularly on a Sunday, they would travel by bus to Stockiemuir where they walked to the 'Whangie', which is a rocky outcrop that falls away from hillside to form a large gulley. This was where they learned to rock climb, as in those days climbing walls didn't exist in the community. This was a popular place for climbers from the Glasgow clubs to hone their rock climbing skills.

Now 18 years of age, Angus worked out of the Waterloo Street delivery office. Later he moved to the Knightswood office and had a delivery section starting at Anniesland Cross and finishing at Knightswood Cross.

Climbing activities were to become more active with weekend trips to the Trossachs, Arrochar Alps, Glencoe, the Cairngorms and Glen Nevis. Two holidays were spent in Skye where the Langside Club camped beside Loch Brittle and spent the days on the Cuillin Hills in Skye. Around this time Angus joined the Garscube Harriers club to be beside his younger brother Neil who was a good junior athlete and footballer. Angus ran all distances between 100 and 400 yards.

At 19 1/2 years of age Angus was discharged from the RNVR to join the Royal Navy at HMS *Raleigh* on 13th October 1958 for National Service. After a short period at HMS *Raleigh*, Angus moved on to HMS *Mercury* near Portsmouth on 3rd November 1958 where he undertook training to become a radio operator 3rd class. After qualifying his rank was changed to A/RO2, as he had an able rate qualification in the RNVR. During his time at HMS *Mercury* he joined the Royal Navy Athletic club in Portsmouth and ran in several Athletic meetings at weekends in a variety of different locations near Portsmouth.

Angus then moved to HMS *Phoenicia* in Malta on 21st August 1959 and served on shore in Valetta at the NATO communications centre, deep underneath the town. Later he was deployed to sea for several months on HMS *Delight*, a daring class destroyer, visiting many different places in the Mediterranean before returning to Malta.

As National Service was coming to an end Angus returned to HMS *Victory*, Portsmouth on 27th March 1960 and was eventually demobbed on 11th May 1960. Angus was now enrolled in the Royal Naval Special Reserve, in which he served from 12th May 1960 to 12th April 1964. He was now able to return to Langside

College to meet up with all his friends and resume his attendance at the club and participate in trips to the hills.

One night at the club Angus became aware of a young lady who had joined in his absence, Janet Donaldson, who worked for Stewart & Lloyds in Jamaica Street as a Comptometer Operator. They became good friends and before long became a partnership. This romance blossomed and eventually they married on 1st March 1963 in the South Church Hamilton.

Family life changed on 2nd December 1964 when twin girls (Carol and Anne) were born.

At work Angus became a Postman Higher Grade working at the main post office in George Square Glasgow. This type of work continued for some time until he responded to an advert for telegraph operators. With his new naval training behind him and his ability to touch type he had no difficulty in taking on this new role within the organisation.

One day when visiting a camera shop in Queen Street Angus was introduced to George L.A. Patrick, who at that time was the Secretary of the Scottish Ornithologists Club in Glasgow. They struck up an immediate friendship and Angus was invited to go to Clarkston where George ran an indoor birdwatching class during the winter period.

George was an excellent tutor with a great knowledge of ornithology he was able to pass on to others. Angus then took the step of joining the Scottish Ornithologists Club (SOC) and joined the Glasgow branch. Within a year or so he was elected to join the committee. Angus remains a member of the SOC and attends meetings in Stirling and participates in annual conferences.

After a year or two he further applied to move to the Overseas Telegraph Department, also in George Square. This he did and stayed in this department until 15th October 1965 when he transferred to the Scottish Prison Service. Angus served as a Prison Officer for 9 1/2 years in H.M.P Barlinnie Prison Glasgow. Whilst serving there, Angus qualified as a Physical Training Instructor at the Pleasance Gymnasiums, at Edinburgh University.

In August 1974 Angus was transferred to the open prison at Penninghame Newton Stewart. He was now able to enjoy the delights of the hills around the area. He took the opportunity to start a birdwatching evening class at the Douglas Ewart High School courtesy of the Extra Mural Department at Glasgow University. Angus, with his friend Russell Nisbet, had worked occasionally as field workers for Charles Palmer, Head of Natural History in the Glasgow Art Gallery and Museum.

This new evening class numbered about 25, all were locals except Geoff Sheppard who had come from Bristol to Stranraer to live. In the summer of 1975 this group of ornithologists all joined the SOC and a new group was formed calling itself the Galloway Group. A school-teacher at the Douglas Ewart Secondary school, Dr Peter Hopkins, became the chairman with Geoff taking on the post of Secretary.

Angus organised the bird watching outings in conjunction with his committee colleagues.

Geoff is today still a link with this group (SOC West Galloway) , but sadly no indoor meetings take place, partly due to the Covid pandemic.

August 1976 saw Angus transferred on promotion to Senior Officer (Physical Training) at the Prison Service

College in Polmont, Falkirk. He had a full range of tasks during his 4 1/2 years at this training establishment. He was the physical training instructor and fully involved in the general training of recruits and in-service training for all ranks. Further promotion to Principal Officer saw Angus moved to Polmont Borstal, which then became a Young Offenders Institution.

In 1987 Angus was transferred to HM Prison Shotts where he continued his service until retiring in December 1993. He was awarded the Imperial Service Order for his meritorious service over 40 years.

After retiring Angus joined the outdoor leaders' staff of C-N-Do Scotland, a walking company based in Stirling, on the premise that he would gain his Mountain Leadership qualification. (In September of 1994 he attended a summer ML course at Glenmore Lodge near Aviemore and in September 1995 was assessed and passed for this qualification. During the next few years, he led some walking holidays in the Wester Ross area including a trip to Skye. One trip on the Southern Upland Way from Portpatrick in the west to Cockburn's Path in the east, always stands out in his mind as one of the great walks in Scotland.

In 1987 Angus's wife Janet was appointed as a Staff Nurse at the RSNH Hospital in Larbert, specialising in mental deficiencies, known now as learning disabilities. Later Janet left the NHS and had 27 years of retirement before succumbing to dementia. For almost 8 years Janet was cared for by the staff in Kinnaird Manor care home, before passing away on 19th April 2020.

On returning to Central Scotland to live and work, Angus took the opportunity to join a Scottish Country dance club. For a while he attended a class in Lenzie near Glasgow taught by a well-known teacher of dance, Duncan McLeod. After a year he joined the Stirling Branch of the Royal Scottish Country Dance society. Soon he was invited to join the demonstration team, and this led to competing in dance festivals and dancing in such venues as the Glasgow Concert Hall, the Albert Halls, Stirling and Dunblane Hydro for several summer seasons with Jim McLeod and his country dance band.

In 1993, '94 and '95 Angus danced at the Edinburgh Military Tattoo as a member of a large team of Scottish country dancers. Later, he danced alongside others, in many videos of Scottish dancing arranged by Stuart and Anita Mackenzie of Independent Video Productions in association with The Dance Video Company. Many of these dance shows and videos have been downloaded to YouTube where they can be viewed.

Angus attended a dance teacher course being run by Dr Alistair MacFadyen, a historian and Scottish country dancer. On completion of the course, he received a 'preliminary certificate'. Angus was invited to teach a country dance class in Braco, Perthshire where he met up with Catherine Petrie an experienced pianist. They spent 18 years together running the class in the village church hall in Braco.

On 10th May 1981 age 42, Angus ran the 2nd People's Marathon held at Chelmsley Wood Solihull in a time of 3 hours 47 mins 46 secs. On 21st June 1981 he ran the Seven Hills of Edinburgh challenge race and successfully completed it. On 30th August 1981 ran the Inverclyde Folk Marathon and completed it in a time of 4 hours 16 mins 58 secs. On 29th August 1982 he ran the

Inverclyde Marathon and completed it in a time of 3 hours 36 mins 34 secs. On Sunday 17th October 1982 he ran the first Glasgow Marathon in a time of 3 hours 39 mins 45 secs. On Sunday 6th May 1984 he ran the Falkirk Half Marathon in 1 hour 39 mins 52 secs. On 28th October 1984 he ran the Falkirk Half Marathon in a time of 1 hour 1 min 20 secs. The same year (1984) he completed a half marathon at Loch Leven Kinross in 1 hour 10 mins.

During his working life in the Prison Service Angus had become an outdoor leader for the Holiday Fellowship, now HF Holidays, a large outdoor walking company offering walking and special interest holidays in many parts of the world.

Angus ran birdwatching holidays on the Isle of Arran for 30 years and during that time also joined their panel of walking leaders. Initially, Angus led on the Isle of Arran and Glencoe, but soon was to be found in the Lake District at HF's house at Derwentbank near Portinscale. Other venues were added to his list, with holidays at Sedbergh, Malhamdale, Monk Coniston and Alnmouth.

Of special note at this time was the opportunity to lead winter walking holidays in the Lake District in 1986. This holiday became a fixture for a number of years as the weather in late February provided sufficient snow and ice to make it worthwhile. Eventually, with the climate becoming warmer, there was insufficient snow to continue offering this holiday.

Angus was later invited to join the panel of leaders for walking holidays abroad and he was soon to be found in the French Pyrenees, Austria, Spain and Iceland. He had also become a member of the Assessment Panel for HF outdoor leaders and was involved with this group for several years.

Angus retired from the leader's panel in November 2007 and received a letter from Andy Berlyn, head of walking operations, thanking him for all his years as a member of the leader's panel. In it he said: '. . . you were one of the few Leaders who were able to excel in all aspects of leading, receiving as good feedback for your countryside information and social activities as for your walking leadership. During your many years of assessing with us we were always able to rely on your good judgement and professionalism as well as your support, friendship and gentle joking. Your dedication and high standards undoubtedly contributed to the current success of our organisation. As well as having many fond memories yourself, I am sure you have enabled many HF guests to harbour similarly wonderful memories for the holidays you have led.'

In July 1994 Angus received an invite from Scottish Natural Heritage to join a Bean Geese working group in Falkirk. He was aware of this species of goose in the Falkirk area and had already met with John Simpson who was monitoring this rare goose in the Carron Valley and the Slamannan Plateau. Angus has monitored the Taiga Bean Goose flock and its distribution in Falkirk and North Lanarkshire with other volunteers since then and continues to do so to this day .

In May of 2003 Angus passed his advanced driving test and became a member of the Institute of Advanced Motorists in the Forth Valley Group, where he joined the local committee as Membership Secretary. On

1st March 2005 he passed his Observer's Test and on 29th August 2006 the Senior Observer Test. By this time Angus had become the chairman of the group and represented Scottish Groups at meetings in England. He retired from observing and his position as Chairman in April 2019.

Angus now enjoys a gentler pace of life with his partner, Denise, who shares his love of the natural world. They enjoy walking, bird watching, wildlife holidays and modern sequence dancing.

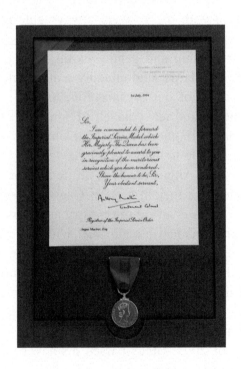

Ronnie and Margaret, The Cobbler c1957

Angus Maciver,
The Whangie c1957

Alistair Beatson,
The Whangie, c1957

Angus Maciver,
HMS Mercury, 1959

Janet with twins
Carol & Anne 1964

Langside CMC, Sgurr Dearg Skye 1959

Edinburgh Tattoo, 1994

Angus and Margaret, 1997

Dunblane Hydro, Stirling dem team c2002

Angus and walking group, Skye 1998

Angus and Denise in the Rocky Mountains 2019